# WISE QUOTES: VOLTAIRE

# (166 VOLTAIRE QUOTES)

Rowan Stevens

*'Optimism,' said Cacambo, 'What is that?' 'Alas!' replied Candide, 'It is the obstinacy of maintaining that everything is best when it is worst.'*

*A man loved by a beautiful woman will always get out of trouble.*

*A State can be no better than the citizens of which it is composed. Our labour now is not to mould States but make citizens.*

*A witty saying proves nothing.*

*All is for the best in the best of possible worlds.*

*All men are born with a nose and ten fingers, but no one was born with a knowledge of God.*



*All men are by nature free; you have therefore an undoubted liberty to depart whenever you please, but will have many and great difficulties to encounter in passing the frontiers.*



*All the reasonings of men are not worth one sentiment of women.*



*Animals have these advantages over man: they never hear the clock strike, they die without any idea of death, they have no theologians to instruct them, their last moments are not disturbed by unwelcome and unpleasant ceremonies, their funerals cost them nothing, and no one starts lawsuits over their wills.*

*Appreciation is a wonderful thing. It makes what is excellent in others belong to us as well.*

*Behind every successful man stands a surprised mother-in-law.*

*Being unable to make people more reasonable, I preferred to be happy away from them.*

*Beware of the words 'internal security,' for they are the eternal cry of the oppressor.*

*Cherish those who seek the truth but beware of those who find it.*

*Common sense is not so common.*




*Dare to think for yourself.*




*Despite the enormous quantity of books, how few people read! And if one reads profitably, one would realize how much stupid stuff the vulgar herd is content to swallow every day.*




*Discord is the great ill of mankind; and tolerance is the only remedy for it.*




*Doctors put drugs of which they know little into bodies of which they know less for diseases of which they know nothing at all.*

*Don't think money does everything or you are going to end up doing everything for money.*

*Doubt is an uncomfortable condition, but certainty is a ridiculous one.*

*Each player must accept the cards life deals him or her; but once they are in hand, he or she alone must decide how to play the cards in order to win the game.*

*Every man is a creature of the age in which he lives and few are able to raise themselves above the ideas of the time.*

*Every man is guilty of all the good he did not do.*

*Everywhere the weak execrate the powerful, before whom they cringe; and the powerful beat them like sheep whose wool and flesh they sell.*

*Faith consists in believing what reason cannot.*

*Fools admire everything in an author of reputation.*

*Fools have a habit of believing that everything written by a famous author is admirable. For my part I read only to please myself and like only what suits my taste.*

*Four thousand volumes of metaphysics will not teach us what the soul is.*

*God gave us the gift of life; it is up to us to give ourselves the gift of living well.*




*God is a circle whose center is everywhere and circumference nowhere.*




*God is a comedian playing to an audience that is too afraid to laugh.*




*He must be very ignorant for he answers every question he is asked.*




*History is the study of the world's crime.*

*History never repeats itself. Man always does.*

*I am the best-natured creature in the world, and yet I have already killed three, and of these three two were priests.*

*I cannot imagine how the clockwork of the universe can exist without a clockmaker.*

*I don't know where I am going, but I am on my way.*

*I hate women because they always know where things are.*

*I have chosen to be happy because it is good for my health.*

*I have lived eighty years of life and know nothing for it, but to be resigned and tell myself that flies are born to be eaten by spiders and man to be devoured by sorrow.*

*I have never made but one prayer to God, a very short one: Oh Lord, make my enemies ridiculous. And God granted it.*

*I have wanted to kill myself a hundred times, but somehow I am still in love with life. This ridiculous weakness is perhaps one of our more stupid melancholy propensities, for is there anything more stupid than to be eager to go on carrying a burden which one would gladly throw away, to loathe one's very being and yet to hold it fast, to fondle the snake that devours us until it has eaten our hearts away?*

*I hold firmly to my original views. After all I am a philosopher.*




*I know many books which have bored their readers, but I know of none which has done real evil.*




*I should like to lie at your feet and die in your arms.*




*I would rather obey a fine lion, much stronger than myself, than two hundred rats of my own species.*




*Ice-cream is exquisite. What a pity it isn't illegal.*

*If God created us in his own image, we have more than reciprocated.*

*If God did not exist, it would be necessary to invent him.*

*If there's life on other planets, then the earth is the Universe's insane asylum.*

*If this is the best of possible worlds, what then are the others?*

*If we do not find anything very pleasant, at least we shall find something new.*

*If you have two religions in your land, the two will cut each other's throats; but if you have thirty religions, they will dwell in peace.*

*If you want good laws, burn those you have and make new ones.*

*In every province, the chief occupations, in order of importance, are lovemaking, malicious gossip, and talking nonsense.*

*In general, the art of government consists in taking as much money as possible from one party of the citizens to give to the other.*

*In the beginning God created man in His own image, and man has been trying to repay the favor ever since.*

*Injustice in the end produces independence.*

*Is politics nothing other than the art of deliberately lying?*

*Isn't there a pleasure in criticising everything and discovering faults where other men detect beauties?*

*It is an infantile superstition of the human spirit that virginity would be thought a virtue and not the barrier that separates ignorance from knowledge.*

*It is as impossible to translate poetry as it is to translate music.*

*It is better to risk saving a guilty person than to condemn an innocent one.*

*It is clear that the individual who persecutes a man, his brother, because he is not of the same opinion, is a monster.*

*It is dangerous to be right in matters on which the established authorities are wrong.*

*It is far better to be silent than merely to increase the quantity of bad books.*

*It is forbidden to kill; therefore all murderers are punished unless they kill in large numbers and to the sound of trumpets.*

*It is hard to free fools from the chains they revere.*



*It is love; love, the comfort of the human species, the preserver of the universe, the soul of all sentient beings, love, tender love.*



*It is not enough to conquer; one must learn to seduce.*



*It is not inequality which is the real misfortune, it is dependence.*



*It is not more surprising to be born twice than once; everything in nature is resurrection.*

*It is not sufficient to see and to know the beauty of a work.
We must feel and be affected by it.*

*It is proved...that things cannot be other than they are, for since everything was made for a purpose, it follows that everything is made for the best purpose.*

*It is said that God is always on the side of the big battalions.*

*It is said that the present is pregnant with the future.*

*It is with books as with men: a very small number play a great part.*

*It requires twenty years for a man to rise from the vegetable state in which he is within his mother's womb, and from the pure animal state which is the lot of his early childhood, to the state when the maturity of reason begins to appear. It has required thirty centuries to learn a little about his structure. It would need eternity to learn something about his soul. It takes an instant to kill him.*

*Judge a man by his questions rather than by his answers.*

*Let us cultivate our garden.*

*Let us read, and let us dance; these two amusements will never do any harm to the world.*

*Liberty of thought is the life of the soul.*

*Life is a shipwreck, but we must not forget to sing in the lifeboats.*

*Life is thickly sown with thorns, and I know no other remedy than to pass quickly through them. The longer we dwell on our misfortunes, the greater is their power to harm us.*

*Love is a canvas furnished by Nature and embroidered by imagination.*

*Love truth, but pardon error.*

*Madness is to think of too many things in succession too fast, or of one thing too exclusively.*

*Man is free at the instant he wants to be.*

*Marriage is the only adventure open to the cowardly.*

*May God defend me from my friends: I can defend myself from my enemies.*

*Meditation is the dissolution of thoughts in Eternal awareness or Pure consciousness without objectification, knowing without thinking, merging finitude in infinity.*

*Men are equal; it is not birth but virtue that makes the difference.*

*Men argue. Nature acts.*

*Men use thought only as authority for their injustice, and employ speech only to conceal their thoughts.*

*Men will always be mad, and those who think they can cure them are the maddest of all.*

*Minds differ still more than faces.*

*My soul is the mirror of the universe, and my body is its frame.*

*No opinion is worth burning your neighbor for.*

*No problem can stand the assault of sustained thinking.*

*No snowflake in an avalanche ever feels responsible.*

*Now, now my good man, this is no time to be making enemies.*

*Of all religions, the Christian should of course inspire the most tolerance, but until now Christians have been the most intolerant of all men.*

*One always begins with the simple, then comes the complex, and by superior enlightenment one often reverts in the end to the simple. Such is the course of human intelligence.*

*One day everything will be well, that is our hope. Everything's fine today, that is our illusion.*

*One great use of words is to hide our thoughts.*

*One merit of poetry few persons will deny: it says more and in fewer words than prose.*

*One should always cite what one does not understand at all in the language one understands the least.*

*Opinions have caused more ills than the plague or earthquakes on this little globe of ours.*

*Originality is nothing by judicious imitation. The most original writers borrowed one from another.*

*Our character is composed of our ideas and our feelings: and, since it has been proved that we give ourselves neither feelings nor ideas, our character does not depend on us. If it did depend on us, there is nobody who would not be perfect. If one does not reflect, one thinks oneself master of everything; but when one does reflect, one realizes that one is master of nothing.*

*Our labour preserves us from three great evils — weariness, vice, and want.*

*Our wretched species is so made that those who walk on the well-trodden path always throw stones at those who are showing a new road.*


*Perfect is the enemy of good.*


*Perfection is attained by slow degrees; it requires the hand of time.*


*Prejudices are what fools use for reason.*


*Reading nurtures the soul, and an enlightened friend brings it solace.*

*Religion began when the first scoundrel met the first fool.*

*Secret griefs are more cruel than public calamities.*

*Sensual pleasure passes and vanishes, but the friendship between us, the mutual confidence, the delight of the heart, the enchantment of the soul, these things do not perish and can never be destroyed.*

*Such then is the human condition, that to wish greatness for one's country is to wish harm to one's neighbors.*

*Tears are the silent language of grief.*

*The art of medicine consists of amusing the patient while nature cures the disease.*

*The comfort of the rich depends upon an abundant supply of the poor.*

*The discovery of what is true and the practice of that which is good are the two most important aims of philosophy.*

*The greatest consolation in life is to say what one thinks.*

*The happiest of all lives is a busy solitude.*

*The heart has its own reasons that reason can't understand.*

*The human brain is a complex organ with the wonderful power of enabling man to find reasons for continuing to believe whatever it is that he wants to believe.*

*The infinitely small have a pride infinitely great.*

*The instruction we find in books is like fire. We fetch it from our neighbors, kindle it at home, communicate it to others, and it becomes the property of all.*

*The interest I have to believe a thing is no proof that such a thing exists.*

*The longer we dwell on our misfortunes, the greater is their power to harm us.*

*The mirror is a worthless invention. The only way to truly see yourself is in the reflection of someone else's eyes.*

*The more a man knows, the less he talks.*

*The more I read, the more I acquire, the more certain I am that I know nothing.*

*The more often a stupidity is repeated, the more it gets the appearance of wisdom.*

*The most important decision you make is to be in a good mood.*

*The mouth obeys poorly when the heart murmurs.*

*The only way to comprehend what mathematicians mean by Infinity is to contemplate the extent of human stupidity.*

*The pursuit of pleasure must be the goal of every rational person.*

*The secret of being a bore is to tell everything.*

*Theology is to religion what poisons are to food.*

*There are truths which are not for all men, nor for all times.*

*There is a wide difference between speaking to deceive, and being silent to be impenetrable.*

*Think for yourself and let others enjoy the privilege of doing so too.*

*Those who can make you believe absurdities, can make you commit atrocities.*

*To hold a pen is to be at war.*

*To succeed in the world it is not enough to be stupid – one must also be polite.*

*To the living we owe respect, but to the dead we owe only the truth.*

*Uncertainty is an uncomfortable position. But certainty is an absurd one.*

*We all look for happiness, but without knowing where to find it: like drunkards who look for their house, knowing dimly that they have one.*

*We are rarely proud when we are alone.*

*We look to Scotland for all our ideas of civilization.*

*We never live; we are always in the expectation of living.*

*We're neither pure, nor wise, nor good; we do the best we know.*

*What can be more absurd than choosing to carry a burden that one really wants to throw to the ground? To detest, and yet to strive to preserve our existence? To caress the serpent that devours us and hug him close to our bosoms till he has gnawed into our hearts?*

*What can you say to a man who tells you he prefers obeying God rather than men, and that as a result he's certain he'll go to heaven if he cuts your throat?*

*What is history? The lie that everyone agrees on…*

*What is tolerance? It is the consequence of humanity. We are all formed of frailty and error; let us pardon reciprocally each other's folly – that is the first law of nature.*

*Whatever you do, crush the infamous thing, and love those who love you.*

*When he to whom one speaks does not understand, and he who speaks himself does not understand, that is metaphysics.*

*When it is a question of money, everybody is of the same religion.*

*Wherever my travels may lead, paradise is where I am.*

*Writing is the painting of the voice.*

*You must have the Devil in you to succeed in any of the arts.*

www.ingramcontent.com/pod-product-compliance
Lightning Source LLC
Chambersburg PA
CBHW071256070526
44583CB00017B/2494